ASSIGNATION
AT VANISHING POINT

Jane Satterfield

Winner
Third Annual Elixir Press Book Awards

ELIXIR PRESS

Assignation at Vanishing Point

ISBN: 0-9709342-9-7

Elixir Press is a non-profit literary organization.

Cover Photo: Modotti, Tina (1846–1942). *Telegraph Wires*. ca. 1925. Platinum/palladium print, 8 15/16 x 6 5/16". Gift of Miss Dorothy M. Hoskins (726.1959). The Museum of Modern Art, New York. Digital image © The Museum of Modern Art, NY/Licensed by Scala/ Art Resource, NY.
Cover Design: Collin Hummel
Layout Design: R. F. Marsocci

Elixir Press
P. O. Box 18010
Minneapolis, MN 55418
www.elixirpress.com
info@elixirpress.com

Acknowledgments

Thanks are due to the editors of the following magazines in which some of these poems first appeared:

Antioch Review: "Requiem"; *Blackbird* (*www.blackbird.vcu.edu*): "Dedication" and "Shugburough Hall"; *Bellingham Review*: "Fugue"; *Crab Orchard Review*: "Antique Dress"; *Elixir*: "The Hour at Hand," "The Kingdom of Heaven Suffereth Violence," "Mercenary Muse," and "The Real Saints"; *Hayden's Ferry Review*: "Mercy" (as "Machinery"); *Indiana Review*: Certainty"; *The Journal*: "War Journal"; *Massachusetts Review*: "Field Service Postcard" and "Instant Combat Kit"; *Notre Dame Review*: "Clamor" and "Stanton Moor"; *Quarterly West*: Ordnance Map"; *Scratch Magazine* (UK): "Coming of Age"; *Seneca Review*: "Bouquets et Frondaisons"; *Sometimes City* (*www.sundress.net/sometimescity*): "Shopping"; *WebdelSol* (*www.delsolreview.com*): "House in Flames," and "Late Letter, Tidmarsh Mill, 19--."

"Requiem" appeared in *The Maryland Millennial Anthology*, edited by Michael Glaser.

Grateful acknowledgment to the Maryland State Arts Council, the Arvon Foundation at Totleigh Barton, the Virginia Center for the Creative Arts, and the Loyola Center for the Humanities for grants and fellowships which aided in the completion of this book.

Thanks to Judith Hall and Frederick Smock who asked for essays that led to many of these poems; thanks, also, to those whose insight and encouragement were invaluable: Ned Balbo, Camille Dungy, Shara McCallum, Penelope Pelizzon, and Ron Tanner.

Special thanks to my family for their support, especially to Paul Satterfield and Kama Dwyer for their generous gift of time.

Assignation at Vanishing Point
Contents

III.

Foreword

> *Anything can be mapped*—the station's electric
> current, ash & chocolate crumbs,
> bedclothes, shards & when the rain relented
> the settled sunshine's lavish garlandry—
>   ("Fugue")

The old mapmakers used to call the blank spaces in maps *Sleeping Beauties*. The lines for roads or rivers stopped there, and no telling exactly what kind of territories these were, *terra incognita*, in other words. In Jane Satterfield's second collection, *Assignation at Vanishing Point*, she may be writing the *Sleeping Beauties*. She gets us from *here* to *here* in poems wherein the present day and History coexist. We do not travel back and forth from *then* to *now*. We exist in both, in one place, like a letter written on the back of another letter, because the speaker manages with her "pocket A-Z" "to translate a path from this place, its famine roads and history of hunger" ("The Rocky Road to Dublin"). She instructs, "Learn from me, if you like, the unstable/the nature of wishes. I sought diversion, a change/of scene" ("Letter From Exile"). The reader follows along Satterfield's lines, to discover whether the speaker arrives at certain *Sleeping Beauties* through flight, through exile, or through pilgrimage … in a style reminiscent of Laura Mullen's in her *Tales of Horror*:

> *here* or *there*, just one moment lost to history,
> where we stood not even an armlength's apart…
> A door through which, "Don't move—"
> One moment then wind
>   ("Fugue")

Most importantly, Satterfield writes the *Sleeping Beauties* between two people:

> this distance we negotiate; the air, countless
> particles seen and unseen, current on which they ride…
> This interval—door, blown window, dusty pane—
> where everything and I am open.
>   ("Erotica")

Negotiating distances, intimate or otherwise, Satterfield's poems contain all the other trappings of travel: the snapshots, film, postcards, phone messages (*"if you have trouble understanding the message/you will be able to hear it again"* ["Coming of Age"]), these ways of keeping the traveling experience long after the experience has passed, these ways of passing the balm of pilgrimage on to others:

> So
> many emotions while touring—*the emissaries, I didn't
> know who to believe*—fog exposing the bright backs
> of the rowers as a voice charged and instructive began

to speak—electric current and unsound ideas—
an altogether ravishing tongue.
                    ("Morning Song")
        And certainly Satterfield's *Assignation at Vanishing Point* is *epistolary*
in the traditional understanding of the term, as the poems are characterized
by the "belle negligence" that epistolary stylisticians carried out purposefully
in the nineteenth century, for aesthetic effect. Ingeniously, in the epistles
"Exile" may be a place or a character letter-writer, the way "History" might
be. We are reading a certain lack of attention to detail, the shredded letter
pulled back together in the speaker's mouth, the *confession without a crime*
from the speaker who has a double in other countries, and can imagine the
double traveling in her own realm. Like the letter, the speaker has a *crisis of
destination* (Derrida). She advises,
                    Who turns his attention from celestial
            to earthly matters will ascend…
            If indeed experience teaches us
            you will name your "exile" more properly
            shackles cast off with good cause
            advancing starry eyed among
            numberless cities and shores
                            ("Letter in Exile—
                            In Protest to a Friend")
Epistolarity booms in the times of the world's crises, says Jacques Derrida in
his *Postcard*; these are times when the reader soaks up realism, or authenticity,
as in wartime. The speaker in *Assignation at Vanishing Point* goes to battle
and acknowledges the distance between a war and its people:
            In strange times who knows where to place desire?
            I'm pissed off—don't know what address to give you.
                            ("War Journal")
Satterfield furthermore demonstrates a distress famous in literature with these
lines … the impossibility of the letter, the possible missed letters of wartime,
peacetime, and those ghosts that Franz Kafka feared would drink up all the
kisses before the letters reached their destinations. The desperate Kafka,
famous for his unconsummated epistolary engagement (or "*marivaudage*"),
could not consider the temporal polyvalence of the letter, whereby the
meaning, according to letter theorist Janet Altman, "is relative not to one
time but to two or more."
        Some of the poems are also erasures wherein live "the comic postcard
suffragette!" and the welcome interruptions of Akhmatova, deBeauvoir, and
Brontë among the cartographers and archeologists. Brontë's voice here is a
satisfying choice because her own Reverend husband censored her letters:
"Arthur says such letters as mine never ought to be kept, they are dangerous
as lucifer matches…." She instructed her letter receivers to *burn* them when
read.
        Satterfield is Franz Hessel's *flaneu* … reading America and the British
Isles…. She is the one who reads a place, and the windows and the displays

and the faces and the trees *become nothing but letters with equal rights, which together make up the words, sentences, and pages of a new book.*

Christopher Columbus determined direction and speed on his sea voyages through *Dead Reckoning*, which meant that he depended on a magnetic compass (or "wind rose") and measured the time it took for saltwater weeds (entangled, infamous) to pass by him on the Sargasso Sea. The method suffered because he knew not his destination. The speaker in *Assignation* knows what she is leaving, yet the point where she is headed *vanishes*. She measures the distances through the stages of an antique dress: first handed down, then roughened, then undone. And we (gladly) are reminded of the famous (imagined pristine) dress of Satterfield's poetical ancestor—Emily Dickinson. From ellipse to dash, divine ear and tongue, and an ear to the divine (with an envy of the focus of saints), Satterfield is like Emily Dickinson in so many ways. We find the caged eroticism of Epistolary Romance in the following Dickinsonesque passages.

I can stop it here—abandon the memory in time.
The landscape. The body—where is the poetic here?
I can push beyond—when I come back I'm mother
and daughter. Three women pose on the packbridge.
The wind. Our sandwiches. Bargain bread. The flowers
blown, the petals spent.
("Shugborough Hall")

*

Clouds pass over in silence—what we cannot speak.
Lips might meet: a thought that maddens.
Light crumbles; flowers flung in the trashcan.
("Double Exposure")

And as in Dickinson's poems, Satterfield's *Sleeping Beauties* resonate with a whispered conversation with a *He*, culminating in her final poem with a version of the meeting she refers to in her title, a meeting with the muse, who, here, is confused with the Other, the lover, the receiver of letters. (Odd how the letters exist because one travels away from the Other. And the letters return to the Other. One never leaves the Other even in leaving. Perhaps theorist Janet Altman is right. Perhaps the letter is *erotic metonymy*.) Perhaps the speaker meets with the object of these letters at *Vanishing Point*, the point being the place of a painful passion flaring and then calming (and flaring again?). Satterfield reminds us that we are travelers even in love. We are entangled *guests*.

It's enough I am in your arms, brief welcomed guest,
breasts bared to endless promises, perfumes.
("Mercenary Muse")

In *Assignation at Vanishing Point*, the speaker's muse is her host.

Michelle Mitchell-Foust

Where there is danger, some
Salvation grows there too.
                    Holderlin

I

One's homeland is not a geographical convention,
but an insistence of memory and blood.
                    —Marina Tsvetaeva

Requiem

In my time I have had to flee twice.
As I fled I knew what I was running from and why.
I was standing at the window of a train watching the platform
sail past me, thinking of the morning's friendly telephone call,
our own clumsily crafted lives.
Who could have guessed the content of my days, whispers,
guesses, real life omitted, just faint glimmers here & there, a hint
of it, some sign, some future which was never to be—
Residue of sleepless nights, little squares of the parquet floor—
my daughter, I felt I had to stay alive for her—
What documents was I keeping & where....
Sometimes, in mid-conversation, silence, followed
with something mundane—"Would you like some tea?" "You're
very tanned," "Autumn came early this year—"
The bookcase, the writing desk, the clock—
chiseling out of this some beautiful & mournful ritual.

On the Circumference & Seized

The memory of the intoxication is surprisingly clear.
Men's faces, some local dish, my lionish hunger—my agitation was infinite…
The street I've seen so often now like a knife cut—the little bar on the harbor,
a brass band, the blaring of car horns exerting its canonical magic…

Such trances, impressions, and prismatic edges, the form of a flower…
For months in my head, evolving like a great drama or a piece of music—
A dark square, before a colonnade or a window—*gloom attended these*
gorgeous spectacles…
Another person, an impassable gulf—on what grounds had I permitted myself
rhythmical bliss, the music that meanwhile kept rising and falling, the rush
and switches of jazz, din of voices at the level of dialect …

His benevolence struck me with sudden violence—A feast into eternity.
Chained from motion, gold coins, ample handfuls of existence—
But for misery, utterances, outward events … amorous joy at the fringes…

…How things withstand the gaze…

Antique Dress

       Seen askance, it's all you've wanted, ever.
A hand-me down
from who knows where, flowered over in
silver embroidery, sheer confection of organza,
someone's fiddly needlework. Slip it on, agree to pose.
Wayward seams uphold—almost—their own against the body's eaves.
And if said model angles, so—here it slips, and here it clings.
       All those studies kindling the flames.

Next thing you know, you're immersed.
The tin bath. An arrangement of oil lamps underneath.
His cold gaze going over your skin.
And your sudden longing for streetclothes, something more serviceable.

The Rocky Road to Dublin

> *The perfect cities are those which I have not spoiled myself*
> *by actually visiting them ... their perfection only remains in*
> *the mind or in the mouth, on paper or film in text or plan*
> *or picture...*
>
> —Simon Armitage

Because of the tide,
    because of the baby,
I didn't get over,
    didn't see my double,
dead-ringer or distant cousin on Dublin streets,
    her shoulderbag stuffed with books,
Independent, pocket *A-Z*.
    In the merry month of May the child stirred and fed,
drifted off to sleep in my arms,
    a look of distance behind her satisfied smile,
little one, expert already in severed connections...

Only minutes past dawn,
    and my double walks abroad in her homeland
as the uncles gather down at the dock
    where touring crowds debark to the drunkard's oratory,
past dawn, the long walk home
    from a lover's room, through the smoking streets,
a rush of wind as mother steps outside to peg the wash,
    bends again to light the hob whose blue flame leaps
at last into being, the dream of how far one has travelled...
    "A rough crossing any time, water slaps the vanishing shore,
    the ferry heaves through wave after wave of iron-grey water,
    salt-wind whipping, sending up spray..."

Past the Post Office, its pock-marked walls,
    to drift along O'Connell Street,
voices rise and fall, *that girl* and *can you credit it...*
    Late autumn and leafrot, the lone piper's notes—
Night mists across Tyrone where once
    "...the bed was hard as rock, my mother shifted
    felt uneasy, lay stiffly awake all night,
    alert to voices rising and falling
    in the distance, growing nearer, receding once again..."
Turning down the road
    and all the way to Dublin town,
calm despite events on the border...Or *wake*

with a start to the clang of keys, the rush of feet,
      as in legacy, white-washed
cottage, the land in someone else's hands,
      mother's grandfather lighting the gas lamps
at the century's start and her almost American sister,
      the rebel songs she learns

to forget, alone at the last in the stacks,
      now bending over an open notebook
where lines are scrawled at intermittent lengths,
      fields hoed to the horizon
to translate a path from this place, its famine roads and history of hunger,
      the violence her brothers have done...
Wind among the trees
      a siren song for the likes of us who wait for the last connection...
Because of the tide, because of the baby,
      while she slips at last into the lecture hall I still have to ask
how much it cost,
      and who's paying?

The Kingdom of Heaven Suffereth Violence

Something's wrong in the heart and in the heavens.
Whirling wants, souls lassoed where they should not be
and something stirs with sudden violence because—

Setting's everything in this skewed picture plane

as these auras emphasize—limbs like wings bent and wavering....
How each angelic has its opposite
caress its brilliant blow ... And in heaven's surface layers,

loops of cadmium, titanium, and lead. Here umber
burnished backwards, here ocher gone amiss.
Heart with absence echoing home.

As in errancy I inhabit: hunger equals industry.

A fetish to finesse. Broker
of bliss and batter, whose *bad*?

What alchemy is here at work.

Late Letter, Tidmarsh Mill, 19—

I have been a hewer of wood & a drawer of water—how can I do a thing?
Coal scuttles, endless meals, visitors, weeks ... my appointed rounds—
The woodblocks on the studio table balanced precariously. Always I move
to approach them, uneasy.

Then the world outside! My garden's one corner, undefiled. But evenings,
for which—alone—I live—the appeal of a scholar's mind, his melodramatic
manner & kiss which (once!) caught me off guard ... When one person
flavours the whole of life—really, I ought to have run a mile. *You've no idea
how ghastly it is* ... green vines, the fruit orchard, gables lattice windows,
electric light—I adored, devoured—while you read at night—

Paintings, the big & devastating love—a path I won't pursue. The
indecency of showing all I have loved!—my nearest & dearest, the
sometimes roughened ivory skin of your hands ... Times I wanted—never
mind....Our evenings, the wonder of it all, conversations, the nerves firing,
firing ... Soaring on these planes of thought, *yr* power of altering me—

If an arbitrary kiss—bookplates, my simple signboards.
—*Nobody*, I think, as much as I...

Say you will remember it.

Archaeology

This is the present—a relic heap—the ground
come clear of history. No sign
of armies, ashes, spines hot still
with arrow shafts.
We skirt the ruined temple's edge in case, alert
for shards, a sudden outcrop.

Always I've wanted to narrow the distance—
clicking off my steps while scanning the hilltop view.
There is the beauty of sunken fields,
the holly and its green armor—
hedge after hedge, inviolate.

The stillness of the obstructing pane,
the ground refusing to give.

Night drifts among the excavations,
the shorn hill's blank gaze.

Instant Combat Kit

For years my father's bag stashed in the car "boot"
leather worn raw, this side of suede,

packed and ready in case—flight suit,
polished boots, an instant combat kit

signed, sealed, to be delivered due east—
the border, the base, the last battle left.

How it hummed, the air, with imminent action,
our house under the flight path, weekend

war games, the enemy out there—
always expected and just within reach

through cross hairs and radar screen.
And though it seemed unique to our age,

apocalypse *now*—blackout, bombardier,
passage of flame (the use of stock photos

is strictly forbidden)—really, what's different?
Just our hands on the switch? In the old

dream of empire, in late afternoon, the story
the child saint raced into, a covert host in his cloak,

is simply a case of street violence and the body
sent into the streets—stand-in and look-out—

a shape divested of meaning. And the blows
coming down until you see you have to forego it,

reason, the right explanation, plot whispering
Did you deliver? What can be reached?

Stanton Moor

When I frequented this place, as I did for some years together, to take exact account of it, staying a fortnight at a time, I found out the entire work by degrees. The second time I was here, an avenue was a new amusement. The third year another. So that at length I discovered the mystery.

—William Stukeley

Off footpaths flecked with frost
while chill wind whirled dark flakes
the better part of days dissolved
in photographing them. I'd skirt
the stone circle's edges, reel off shots,
think of immolation, sacrifice.
Before me on this ancient ground,
jagged teeth against dense sky, razor-edged
to the touch. No trace of souls who'd settled,
just scattered remnants of lost inhabitants, the countless cairns
spread far as the eye could see...
I watched the snow, the thousand intersections and collisions
of light and time and flesh and space
that fuse and fall and fall away, same snow
filling fissures, hairline cracks which leave us
at a loss, longing for kindling, fire—
cooled heat only flesh can hold.

Fugue

I dreamed the habitual emigre dreams of returns and entrapment.
—Jan Novak

Where spring light brands the floor
I'm stringing wash along the lines.
Dusk's street noise is Jagger's thrum on vinyl
& the last light slaps the blinds while I dress in deepening dark.
If I dress & get
to the door ... or, there is a door through which—
"don't move," there is a door, & when we get to
waking life's incendiary air,
I'm unlaced, led by the hand up from the underground—If I dress...
But the origin of the map is lost to history—

Crosscut to broadcasts,
shifting borders. At the phone box
agreeing, "I'll be over."
At first it seems a sentence,
here or *there*, one finds a way...
some relation, the intervening ocean,
a sketch, some sense of place—

Light on the ring road, my room
in another country where the letter—scrawled—
must make the last post, all my attempts
to survey the whole in just proportions—

here or *there*, just one more moment lost to history,
where we stood not even an armlength's apart...
A door through which, "Don't move—"
One moment then wind

blowing off the Thames, a long walk home
through Camden Town...

—We had reached the rim of the upper world.
When I stopped expecting   I saw   in some
relation to each other—*here* or *there*, a *history*—
dead limbs taken up   ignited by the flames
in your hands & falling as we race
to where music fades to static...

*   *   *   *   *

The tube station's hissing tracks.

Charged lines to somewhere else. Platforms of the possible.
Change for fare, a pocket *A-Z*. Mind the gap
& skirmish with the dark, through tunnels
where dossers play, on to borrow books.
Trench coat & slashed-on smile: "I'm not looking, lost."
    Push past the place where tulips flared
beyond the bedroom door. An angle of repose,
speaking from a prone position…"What will be is not;
& what would be; what was, what might
have been …" Disruption and delay…

    Heading out
into the rain as traffic stalled along the streets.
Downtown the homicide & clean up crews.
    Some extreme attraction   the afternoon's
tableau of flesh   Smoke stains on the pavement   bloody aftermath….
    Seasons shuttered past. A gallant gesture, a glass
or two, paths across thighs, lips, eclipse,
iced streets & "banish it …"

            I wake and won't
know where I am

                    some sense of place & all my attempts—
"Not that, not there" & crackling in the wind,
the yellow caution sign…

        *   *   *   *   *

    What is the relation, *here* or *there, a system*
of parallels & all my attempts—a sudden & difficult
    trying to steer in the cold, smoking streets—from you I hid— &
there is a door & a room where we cannot live, the origin—
without which it is impossible—

        Anything can be mapped—the station's electric
current, ash & chocolate crumbs,
bedclothes, shards & when the rain relented
the settled sunshine's lavish garlandry—

        *   *   *   *   *   *

Where time bites along my shoulder blade
        a system of parallels & all my attempts—

14

I passed packed pubs
along Ironmarket, scent of mince & the street
    full of rain & rain splashing stone … insane desire to be somewhere else
your key in my hand … & up ahead a door through which—

Guards cradled automatics. Strangely silent, the airport
    exhausted its repose.

    —not only to get somewhere but to know
where you have been—

fear   the engines revving outside—
    I had been looking—the wind, *the origin, some sense—*
& all my attempts
    the inconveniences of place & circumstance,
& something's lost or I'm losing—the wires pulled
    the connection missed

      & there is a door, a garden, an origin:

something said in passing,
    night blazing at your back, the stars
        in strange design—

Dedication

The whole town stands covered in ice.
The trees, the walls, the snow
are as though under glass.
As I stepped down into the cellar, the lantern
started to smoke.
Everything went dark before my eyes.
It's not pain I fear, nor being alone—
but these phantasms—
cool touch of hands, and after, words of consolation.
Among flower kiosks last summer,
an ancient sound chimed from distant bells.
A sudden premonition: my ruined home.
The flowers of a meeting I missed
lie trembling on my breast,
a fire neither fear nor oblivion can touch.
Insomnia, the lost lilac, made me think of you—
the blue carriages of the metro, buried under snow,
stuck a long time between stations.

Field Service Postcard

I have some vague idea of throwing clothes in a suitcase
and beginning to walk away. *Surely someone so clever*
could think her way out of this. Fear and its milder brothers,
dread and anticipation. I am sick/wounded/going on well.
So much for humorous restraint in describing unparalleled terrors.
What the lark usually betokens is that one has got safely through
another night. Summer, a string of bright days,
the same resignation and acceptance.
I received your letter/telegram/
parcel/am being sent down to the base.
Wildflowers in bloom, the country on the verge of chaos.
I have not heard from you lately/in a long time.
Take "the character"'s degree of moral paralysis, an argument with life
and its chances, destiny and its decrees—
Eventually one will act—the tablets of memory,
rose and sweat, blood and rum. *The pink dress, I thought I should not—*
The date and signature of the sender—When "she" acts it is because—
all sentences not required will be erased.

Shugborough Hall

Staffordshire, England

The flag is flying over the smog-grimed walls of Shugborough, seat of the earls of Lichfield. The earl, apparently, is in residence. We have driven almost a mile along a one-track road through the amusements the National Trust has designed to raise revenue, the farm park, for instance, the plant shop. Littered along the expansive view are the remnants of Capability Brown's handiwork—a pagoda, temple, hunting lodge, the evenly spaced arrangements of English oak that seem to hug or hover along the ground, depending on your view.

We have come because we like the walk—a gravel footpath which follows the river, whose sinuous curves were artfully engineered to please the eye. We do not, will not, venture inside. Perhaps the price is prohibitive, or we know what such estates are like. On the other side of the bank, fevered with daffodils, a herd of cattle lazes in the wan English sun, vast machines moving their hulks across the pasture. Languid, almost inert. I know the future—its steady tug, dark water, storms to sail through.

The earl and his family arrange themselves on the terrace. No one is after a close up of them. The fountains and footpaths are expressly off-limits. The rose garden is not yet in bloom. The gravel makes my footing uncertain.

I can stop it here—abandon the memory in time. The landscape. The body— where is the poetic here? I can push beyond—when I come back I'm mother and daughter. Three women pose on the packbridge. The wind. Our sandwiches. Bargain bread. The flowers blown, the petals spent.

Wintering

The worst winter in ages—pipes freeze, nerves fizzle,
tempers flare then even more descends
as one more snowfall starts, a swirl of flakes

over laden boughs, what is already
perilous … The slushy ruts thaw, refreeze,
and once again the work of digging out

as the urban flat takes on the isolation
of the moors. Still one lost soul
will brave it, drop round for a drink and so the story

detonates—what lies ahead (the branches out),
the ground below (sterile, demythologized),
the hidden flame at the heart of the house

and the slight girl who slips out, well aware
the lock is turned behind her. Hears the elevator's
tension cables, just that clattering there.

II

Who lays the crumbs of food that tempt you? Towards a person you never considered. A dream. Then later another series of dreams.
—Michael Ondaatje
The English Patient

I had been hungry, all the Years—
My Noon had Come—to dine—
—Emily Dickinson
#579

House in Flames

We stood on the terrace talking about *Anna Karenina*,
her bearing, azure shawl, distracted look. "Come closer," he said,
and when I looked back,
the house was plunged in flames. Screams
from inside as moonlight silvers the slats—
what does this explain, is the torture exquisite?
Desired somehow? Blood and bandages, "Is it all right?"
And when thought runs ahead of the thinker, will the last link
in the chain reveal who gets in the way of your progress—
The laborer, the squire, what to tell the tutor—
  —rough hand, silk thigh, I felt an obligation,
  rough hand, silk, I felt—

dulled by accusations, drama's nineteenth
century dress.

Double Exposure

This maddening thought—lips might meet.
What we can't speak we pass over in silence.
Winter sticks in the makeshift sky, the concrete

outside ground down to crumbs.
Trees maintain their terse positions, shyness
in an instant struck over and over—

Clouds pass over in silence—what we cannot speak.
Lips might meet: a thought that maddens.
Light crumbles; flowers flung in the trashcan.

As clouds meet like lips in silence,
flowers passed over in silence, shyness
flung into the trashcan.

We madden with what we cannot speak—

The Demon Lover

The attraction was in the script's charged air:
the path to the ruins, past the waterfall
and through the wind's incessant song.
The mastiff alongside, its bared teeth nicking flesh.
        Like truth stepping out of a shiny black Benz,
he took her aside, *unredeemed and unswerving*
in his arrow-straight course to perdition,
        bolster against the sometimes blue
suffocating skies, potatoes to peel, weight of the German text.

Neither saw *the rocks bristling far off in the bed*
of the stream, the breakers boiling at their base, a future broken into
whirl and tumult, foam and noise.

Proposals in the dark alley, sunken bridal veil.
The real dark shores all the more inviting because.

The Hour at Hand

The hour was at hand when we began to believe
we knew all about burning, knew an explosion's shock waves
can be felt and survived. But how does this happen—
requiems & rusted tanks, grim script
of solvent, superstores & the sound
of this American girl describing the clouds
was the voice of the soul in hollow places.
The hour was the theater of the unsaid, the infinitely more *troublant*,
noise arriving like gestures made at lightspeed—
a whole dimension opened to dispute.

Mercy

Suddenly there's no shade, no screen and spring's
some vast machine we're at the mercy of, everywhere
limbs bared and brought down. Honeysuckle
takes over the hedge, covert pleasures,
tentacle snares. This congress of crows
over the lawn, you don't give a damn
what they argue. The holly now bronzed—
one rendition. The pane opens out
on a garden not ours for admittance,
stone benches, the herbs
staked and bound, more of this building's faded grandeur...
I want a field at the end of it,
behind whisky light, something charged and magnetic
where obstacles are of no account—

No orange blossom, no veil.

Assignation at Vanishing Point

(I)

When the wind came from the east
their trouble became more pronounced.
So it was no surprise he appeared in a dream,
eyewitness history of the world
resigned to his misfortunes...
I was so rapt on reaching those clearings,
swayed by whatever played out below—
His eyes, bouquets of deadly nightshade ... I forgot the bracelets
I'd placed down beside me, mist now giving
the world-out-there an almost abstract sheen...
Like the graves of the aristocracy long hidden from view—*why did
you come back, what did you hope to find?*

(II)

This is not what I meant—
the larcenous brushwork of light.
The carpet of flowers is a dark abyss.

Heat obscures the knotted path, where it leads...
And the forest impresses itself on the eye,
bronzed columns of beech a blotter for sky,
that atmospheric old scroll, imprint
of birds and beasts at the edge.

     Garments cast off. Lies. An elaborate smoke screen...

...And beyond this—the sun
eclipsing the snares.
Still coupled and ready to strike—

Certainty

Someone who, dreaming, says "I am dreaming," even
if he speaks audibly in doing so, is no more right than
if he said in his dream 'it is raining,' while it was in fact
raining. Even if his dream were actually connected with
the noise of the rain.

—Wittgenstein

I cannot seriously suppose—

By which is meant—

An arm around me as in *the likelihood*—

A rusted fence barricades a view—

Bear with me one moment—

Admittedly one can imagine—

I can't be making a mistake—*I was with him today*—
Is that something one can forget

The question doesn't arise
if someone says *I have a body*

One is often bewitched by a word

I am inclined. But — — —

Even a proposition like this one
…living in England … it is not a mistake

…on the other hand, what do I know of *the country*

Might I be shaken by things such as I don't
dream of at present?

This would happen through a kind of persuasion

Some slip of the tongue

At some point one has to pass
from explanation to mere description—

As in sirens. Sound of the city below.
& your breath beside me.

As in distance ever blooming. Hum & channel click.
One is often bewitched—

As in *but otherwise must honor—*

The clock face turned away.

Admittedly one can imagine a case—

Which we are experiencing & *No, after you.*

The unavailability of which
a hole in the vault of heaven
more than beginning to get under my skin

After the "awakening" one never has doubt
which was imagination & which was reality

      *—does my phone call to New York
strengthen my conviction earth exists*

      to be in doubt & *will it*, chattering away

To be sure there is some justification
but justification comes to an end

With the proposition "it was written"
—assurance is employed

& thus expunge the sentences that don't
get us any further

—some slip ... *so far as I can judge*

Ordnance Map

Driving while talking, shifting erratically & not pausing to ask, *is this the turn or am I on track*, & you there in your seat, unswerving, along for the ride—just what is holding you in & does it matter here where May light flays the wide streets? God knows how quickly I'd trash it, this car, motion's slick photofinish, exquisite hum of belief—want it up-ended? Want it in flames? & we're stepping on dangerous turf where X first bent to the bootleg, where voice is the dream of the right route which puts words in my mouth, just something more for the pain, coal fires in August, mislaid ordnance map, the locust in bloom, the scent of which is said to *assault*, all those sea-bitten, rust-eaten tanks, the shattered histories you love so much as the engine boils over & nothing translates.

Coming of Age

A sense of overload trying to be a person of substance,
killing time, crash course in American lit,
a closed door still the height of bliss.
My appearance I refused to take seriously,
speech a device for saying nothing born when
something goes slightly adrift...
A nameless anxiety colors the air: "You can't
just go to his place, drink soda, page through *die Zeit*."
Desk diaries, unfiltered fags. *Second-hand, third-hand,*
received and reified—the ecstasy, excitement of the world
                                    and when it cracked:
a distant voice through the machine—
if you have trouble understanding the message
you will be able to hear it again.

Metaphysical

for Catherine, 5/21/95, Stoke-on-Trent, England

Because I couldn't see, no story took shape—
I sat still in this absence. Heard film on its spindle,
the machine taking up slack, events at a rate I failed
to comprehend ... Some conflagration, birds taking flight, just words
on the wall, slapped down, a *spiel*. Shouts around me, a song
going up, Manchester United winning a goal & I walked *a grove untouched
by human hands where water falls from dark springs, the interlacing
boughs banished from sunlight*—

Because I believed there was escape in intelligence (dear buffer zone!),
the trees rustled among themselves, the yew
fell & rose again. Through fog, attendants shadowed around me...
A curtain with gaps, then "something more for the pain."
No help & no voice & *behold*
a human shape on the brink of a lake & the valley thrown
into relief as the greased canal gave up its sheen &
the stylized graves slipped out of view...

The Real Saints

> *Pain without marks is like speech without writing,*
> *doomed to pass into oblivion.*
>   —Maud Ellman, *The Hunger Artists*

And why not envy them, manacled, in place,
those who bow to impulse, the thousand
variants of harm, self-sacrifice and the body

offered up as flames lick the tallow feet.
Who wouldn't want to bend before
the lacerating rod, go down on knees
before your god, idea of god, restless and

absolute. This desire to be marked and stigmatized…
Such hunger leaves one helpless,
wanting it all ways at once, lashed to earth and sent beyond—

Tell me, will I always walk this moonlit corridor
of pain—How to learn to love it? *Want it?* When not one

pang brings her, nuzzling, nearer—museling, darling daughter.

Hope

Klimt

All afternoon the painter's addressing
the riddle of flesh
in an angle of light.

Fiddly work to get it right,
now that love stands Atlas-backed
under astonishing weight.

Hope in their native tongue's this *expectancy*—
where they've lain & what lies in wait.

So much for masks, the gilded screen,
the carpet of flowers—
the instant of eros
where laundress = goddess—
a subject
made & unmade.

Harm hovers, a circle
of crones on the horizon.
Still, her glance is unabashed
& still aroused. Meeting his.
That practiced, penetrating gaze:
strokes terrible & true.

—Mistress of heaven, dust, debris…
If she's naked now,
what will she take off next?

Erotica

There's nothing so erotic as a kind
Of understanding....
                    —David St. John

Not so much these fallen blossoms—
"intimate as underthings"—bulbs spent and blown
across a rumpled bed,
camisoles strewn about,
the coming undone—
but gravity and grace,
sky-map of planets, stars throbbing & in place,
this distance we negotiate; the air, countless
particles seen & unseen, current on which they ride...
This interval—door, blown window, dusty pane—
where everything & I am open.

III

*The beauty of the world has two edges, one of laughter,
one of anguish, cutting the heart asunder.*
—Virginia Woolf

Letter From Exile: *On This Transitory World*

Learn from me, if you like, the unstable
the nature of wishes. I sought diversion, a change
of scene, but was seized
with a longing to see again the familiar hills, groves
                                        carpeted with green,
the ever resonant rocks—the charm of the place
and some inward spur compelled me, sober reason
could not hold me back … Somehow I incurred
the displeasure—I will not dwell on the bitter theme …
                                        I came here
with my eyes open, not by some hazard of fate,
not the awareness of what I should gain and what
I should sacrifice … long custom, second nature,
lines and nets in the river, the sweetness
of my transalpine home … of this I have spoken at length…
        …Rough rustic pleasures, the meaning of friendship,
worthiest of all causes in this transitory world.

Madonna in Repose

The fête was over, the lamps were fading—but not all had been satisfied with friendship, its calm comfort and modest hope. I took refuge in the garden, the lavish garlandry, and found myself charged with a role—a piece of extravagance I could ill afford. A thousand objections—the limited time, the public display, my calculated daily attire: *The use of tempting such a catastrophe!*

Chains of flowers and *more than I could swallow* … First in a whisper and then aloud … *If the noon shone, if only there were stars* … When the prayer bell rang I was fugitive, recklessly altered— As for dreams, my child, those afternoons—

Do not let me think of them too often, too much, too fondly.

Study With a Line From Sartre

Time was something sunstruck—

Promise branding the walls like the beauty of the letter not sent:
"Love, the louvered doors let in too much light!"

Later, even the air's confusing.
The river the color of slate. Instructive and still.
Gunmetal blue for sky—
And shades of something else—
Dark music which drives me to desire, distraction.

Think of the others who aren't afraid
to look up, think of the scraps from the feast.
The glare from the kleigs? A fact that wouldn't deter.

This probably isn't how blindness starts,
vision dulling to grey, the café a washout...

People walk out of nightmare and into the street.
Is *that* what you wanted to say?

Shards & Scripts

So busy and dissipated of late that I have delayed writing.
On Monday, I shopped 'till I flopped. Yesterday, a fifteen-mile walk.
Anxious (often) steps through a most awful wilderness of bare moors
toward a ghastly place—crumbly cliffs and a hinterland of slum.
And last month—the shires. A maiden aunt drove me melancholy mad.

These protests we have planned—who knows...
One risks—and the specter—the comic postcard suffragette!
I should mention one speaker astounds. A surprising facility
for saying the first thing that comes into her head. The audience reeled
but adored her.

Knocked down and trampled—
my trouble was both tragic and ludicrous, but it's over now.

Of course my life's in a tangle. Entirely my fault.
This week's issue's past due, a panegyric ... still, it's decent pay. But I like to get
the record straight. *Will* people see through this skullduggery!

    ...I am remembering your dinner party with passion in this dreadful place.
I concentrate on it in the middle of lectures on Labour 'till I feel
a little happier.

    Too weary to work and now I must pay...

I do regret that concert (not the one I went to—which I loved—
but the one I cannot go to)—

Scary Interface

I like the prospect of a long walk,
the *allée défendue.*
Lit a fire, took out my books,
field flowers, paper whites, mere mortal benediction.
Another day's hard riding, rapt and beyond reach...
And when she drifted out of depth,
whose hand whose hand...
The keen still cold of the morning was succeeded
by a heavy firmament. The snow settled, no bouquet.
To whom do I address myself?
Trackless wastes and message trail—
It was like
      it was like
           it was ... And even at this distance:
Those moments authorship eluded us—
your eyes hazed jungle green,
singed stars, lamps and blessings, your beautiful face.

Bouquets et Frondaisons

Lest the effort of answering
overmaster self-command...

...The effectiveness
of his underpinnings.

—Having fed to satiety...

Whim & whereabouts.
A destiny knots & catches.

Aspects. Aspidistra.
Nerves wrong & humor crossed.

On the outskirts & ignited by flame.
Licking my lips over *auld lang syne*.

Cataclysm & camps.
... My project ... which was to please...

Revel of hips. Whips, organza.
Out on the moor & eventide.

Bracken & thorn. Slash marks on skin.
Often, with ease.

Fences. Those feral lines.
... when the affections play a part...

Floorboards of an empty room.
The corner of a field.

A wavering light.
My logic.

Schloss Kammer

Klimt

Under the archway, the promise of shade,
as an avenue gilded and leading me in.
So far from duty, streets I knew,
the garden's simmering perfumes.

I remember heat, bees drifting through
the luminous screen. How they glittered,
the poppies—an army of decorous leaves.
A spread of flame to the touch.

Letter From Exile: *On the Origin of Souls*

I must repeat what I have often said—
the villas soaked with sun ought to leave me indifferent
but what were to me now the futilities
of an individual past,
the long campaigns of my life…
      I won't speak of the celestial origin of souls
stars and heavenly bodies
secluded fonts, mighty rivers
hearts long fixed on heaven…
I had suspected, and now I learn—
Your affection, my own affairs—wandering, never
settling down, I migrate and return—
More of this at another time.
      Let others ascribe their peace to what they will…
Violent seas have swept me elsewhere.
Which must be, for the moment, my reply.

Shopping

All the brides were out buying
satin shoes, handbags of sleekest,
brightest, whitest leather, polished
to a mirror sheen, compact and having space enough
for mother's lipstick, cigarettes…
All the brides, so sure, deciding *you're not carrying
that down the aisle* … All the brides were out buying,
trying, days of lying, *looks good*,
it'll work, I promise, brides
knowing what they're buying,
days of trying, finery assembled,
a kind of scrying … I was smiling,
taking back shoes, a bag, no use denying
what would and wouldn't work.
A mother's scrying: all those days
of trying, taking back
smiles, finery, lies I was carrying…
        What was *I* buying? Trying days,
no more buying shoes, bags,
finery, a smile's mirror sheen
compact enough to carry all those days
as *mother*, trying, finery assembled, a kind of scrying
taking back *I promise*, the *I'll's* a husband had been buying.
So I paused there, looking on and smiling,
trying lipstick shades
the brides beside me were not buying.

Morning Song

One may remember lush pastures with little more than regret, but the candles were set in a bowl before bed and on waking that morning I found they were out. The gap between reason and action is great—*starve now, explain later*; still I felt I must rouse myself while walking old paths through the dim flat, Cambridge, cloud cover, rain. Incense of absence, Master reverie … Morning is the mythic's worked gold brought to light, a movement through waves, surface shimmer, suggestion & hidden depths—So many emotions while touring—*the emissaries, I didn't know who to believe*—fog exposing the bright backs of the rowers as a voice charged and instructive began to speak—electric current and unsound ideas—an altogether ravishing tongue.

War Journal

In strange times who knows where to place desire?
I'm pissed off—don't know what address to give you.
The weather's filthy. Impossible to make any plan.
Last night, a sensational storm, lasting for hours.
It was truly splendid, the blast furnaces spitting fire
to the heavens. I'm not doing much thinking.
I grabbed a bicycle, ready to go for a real ride.
Once I ran into a dog, another time two older ladies,
but for the most part it was a glorious performance.

This morning for the first time, the weather's grey.
I passed some armored cars laden with Germans.
Tank crews, I think, with their black uniforms,
big berets and death's head insignia.
I thought I caught sight of someone else snatching you up,
so I stepped back hastily. Heart-rending
to see them with my own eyes—someone—
taking delivery of you. I wandered about the platform
for a moment, desolate. Then I left and went down.
There was a village fête in progress, which seemed like an insult!

Amid all this gloom, you no longer think of possible accident.
But every so often you're struck by the obvious fact you're mortal.
So much can crumble, your passage through the air becomes supernatural.
You should know first that I'm calm, blocked against all memory.
Over brandies, the peak of happiness—as if you'd touched me.
I've promised myself to put plenty away.

The Pure Life

Clare, of Assisi

Smolder of noon on shutters, sills, hedges, hills, and the square's golden statuary—
And off in the distance, the horizon's fires, whole fields where men move in unison
to beat back the flames, tongues lit and wavering, then Angelus sealing shut
the cries of merchants, servants, the endless, milling crowds—

To give more light than anyone!—And then, a voice—mesmeric. As in street
and summons, going through the door of the dead … Whose hands—
once—sheared my skin. *I have so little, Lord, to offer*—only birdsong slicing
air, a little wind whipping the dust, rasp of rushes, bouquets and herbs along
the road, the upraised palms of supplicants in procession…

Prayer bell and dream of days, dress I shed, the meals I begged—denied.
A life of what?—standing outside one's self, the chosen poverty and pure
life, meadow in which I moved, *worthless servant, little plant* … Fever in
which I moved, patches of pure delight, a scented store on which to feed…

From her who hath been long shut up—

—Spring. And music.

Letter From Exile: *In Protest to a Friend*

Now you call life a wretched exile
I think you have forgotten "the world"
I don't deny the sweetness
something planted deep in our minds
this affection and more—
       A vast number have spent
their lives in perpetual wandering...
It *is* a pleasant virtue to stay in one's own
fields, to know the qualities of one's own soil,
the water and the trees the sowing seasons
and rakes and grub hoes and plows—
       To return to your exile,
the dark clouds of the present
everywhere happy voices raised in cheers
and applause let me say what I think
these terms signify in common speech,
a malignant star, your own weak appreciation—
       Who turns his attention from celestial
to earthly matters will ascend...
If indeed experience teaches us
you will name your "exile" more properly
shackles cast off with good cause
advancing starry eyed among
numberless cities and shores

Clamor

When war breaks out it's always bad news
for the guest of the house. Armed bands
operate on their own account while those
with famous bloodlines stay in the background
where tea on the terrace is maintained at great expense.
Lovers meeting one last time
under sun, among olive trees and lemons
rise to fall again and feel
the drama of connection. The best
pastoral intentions
ignite from inside, *I have stepped*
into a minefield, I have to walk with great care.
Irrational brawls and optional extras,
exile under darkening skies, another tale
of missed connections....
To this day I can distinguish the bark of flak
from the scream of an aerial bomb...
In the late clamor of pots and pans
the one who is turned away
will remember most the brief extinction
of their lives, paths the sleepy
tongue can take, lips stained with local wine—
afternoons the body was a blessing.

Mercenary Muse

Palatial hunger, poor dear and heart's love—*alas*—
when January lacerates the soul, to what
will you resort? Another's room? And dreams
of Azores, after? Who will hear your riddles—
endless—out?—the desolating nights—snow after snow?
...As for our acrobatics, scarce to be believed...
Take these apparitions
and your temporary laughter—or pour champagne at
a vulgar rate...
It's enough I am in your arms, brief welcomed guest,
breasts bared to endless promises, perfumes.

Notes

Requiem draws on descriptions of Akhmatova's daily life described in Lydia Chukovskaya's *The Akhmatova Journals* (Volume 1: 1938–1941). New York: Farrar, Strauss, Giroux, 1994.

On the Circumference & Seized draws on accounts of ecstatic intoxication appearing in Thomas deQuincey's "Confessions of an English Opium Eater" and Walter Benjamin's "Hashish in Marseilles."

Lines 2-3 of **Antique Dress** are from the Velvet Underground's "All Tomorrow's Parties." In order to paint his version of Ophelia, John Everett Millais had his model lie in a tin bath filled with water which was lit and "warmed" from beneath by a few scattered oil lamps.

The Rocky Road to Dublin: On returning to England from Dublin, my brothers reported having seen my double, a particularly resonant claim as my mother's family originated in Northern Ireland. During summer holidays in the 1950s, my mother and her parents traveled to her grandfather's farm in Omagh, County Tyrone; her accounts of these visits reflect the family's discomforting awareness of Tyrone's longstanding Republican loyalties. The poem overlays my mother's accounts with my imagined account of a possible "sister" life as this "double" walks through her city, one known to me solely through literary accounts.

Italicized lines in stanza four are borrowed from Seamus Steele's 1954 account of a strip strike which appears in Tim Pat Coogan's *The IRA: A History*. Boston: Roberts, Rinehart, 1993.

The Kingdom of Heaven Suffereth Violence is the title of a painting by Evelyn de Morgan (1850–1919), depicting a chaotic choir of angels ascending into heaven.

Late Letter, Tidmarsh Mill, 19— owes a debt to Frances Spalding's "Painting Out Carrington" (*The New Yorker*, December 18, 1995).

Instant Combat Kit During the Cold War, personnel in airlift squadrons stationed at Andrews Air Force Base were required to sustain military preparedness even when off-duty. In the event of a national security threat requiring sudden mobilization, squadrons could be instantly dispatched to an unnamed base at the edge of the "free world."

Catholic schoolchildren are often taught stories (probably apocryphal) of youthful martyrs who carried the Eucharist from one Christian community to another in the later days of the Roman Empire, meeting their death in the streets as a result of their refusal to give over the emblem of their faith.

Stanton Moor is a gritstone plateau in Derbyshire which contains a remarkable concentration of prehistoric sites; the best known is Nine Ladies Stone Circle, a name which reflects the folk belief that "standing stones" are the frozen remains of renegades punished for "dancing" or otherwise breaking religious prohibitions. William Stukeley was an amateur archeologist, the first to excavate and study Stonehenge.

Fugue's use of details and phrases regarding the history of cartography are drawn from John Noble Wilford's *The Mapmakers*. New York: Knopf, 1981.

Dedication is inspired by Lydia Chukovskya's account of Akhmatova's efforts to sustain her writing under political persecution.

The Field Service Postcard originated as front-line communique during World War I. Standardized language ensured military security and provided soldiers with "ready-made" phrases that effectively distanced the horrors of trench warfare. The poem draws on material in Charlotte Brontë's *Villette* (New York: Bantam, 1986) detailing Lucy Snowe's inability to reconcile her internal struggle against and desire for human attachment.

Material from Brontë's novels are adapted in other poems as well, among them **The Demon Lover**, **Madonna in Repose**, and **Bouquets et Frondaisons**. **Madonna in Repose** paraphrases a line from Emily Bronte.

Italicized phrases in lines 9–10 of **Coming of Age** are borrowed from Greil Marcus's essay "Born Dead." *Ranters and Crowd Pleasers: Punk in Pop Music, 1977–1992*. New York: St. Martin's Press, 1993.

Italicized lines in **Metaphysical** are from Didorus Siculus' descriptions of Celtic ritual sites; other descriptions are drawn from Tacitus' *Germania*.

Hope is one of a series of Klimt's paintings of an expectant model. Klimt was known to have exploited his models sexually as well as economically; the juxtaposition of maternal beauty and spectral imagery in the paintings conveys a terror of female eroticism.

Erotica's quotation in line two is from Eavan Boland's poem, "The Briar Rose." *Outside History*. New York: W.W. Norton and Company, 1990.

The **Letters from Exile** are inspired by letters of exiled writers, especially Petrarch, Seneca, and Plutarch. Robinson, Mark: *Altogether Elsewhere: Writers on Exile*. Boston: Faber and Faber, 1994.

Shards & Scripts draws on material from the *Collected Letters of Rebecca West*. New Haven: Yale University Press, 2000.

Scary Interface is the title of an installation by Neil Goldberg first exhibited at New York City's P.S. 122 Gallery and appeared under the heading "Keeping in Touch With Nature" in *Harper's*, Vol. 291, No. 1745, October 1995. Italicized lines are paraphrases of lines from *Villette*.

Schloss Kammer was the name of Klimt's summer retreat, the subject of several landscape studies.

War Journal draws on material in deBeauvoir's *Letters to Sartre*. New York: Arcade, 1993.

Italicized language in **Clamor** paraphrases lines of Hans Magnus Enzensbergers's essays on nationalism. *Civil War*. London, Granta Books, 1994.

Mercenary Muse is a homophonic translation of Baudelaire's "La Muse Venale."

Other Titles From Elixir Press

Nomadic Foundations
Sandra Meek
0-9709342-3-8 • $13

Flow Blue
Sarah Kennedy
0-9709342-5-4 • $13

Monster Zero
Jay Snodgrass
0-9709342-6-2 • $13

Circassian Girl
Michelle Mitchell-Foust
0-9709342-2-X • $13

Distance From Birth
Tracy Philpot
0-9709342-1-1 • $13